KU-618-489

# Friendship Bracelets

**Liz Unger and Clare Mayhew**

hinkler

# About this Book

This book contains everything you need to know to create some beautiful and unique friendship bracelets.

## To make great friendship bracelets you will need:

- Embroidery thread in a range of colours
- Coloured beads
- Bracelet wheel
- Bracelet charms
- Clasps
- Scissors
- Masking tape
- Safety pins
- Bull clip
- Ruler
- Hardback book

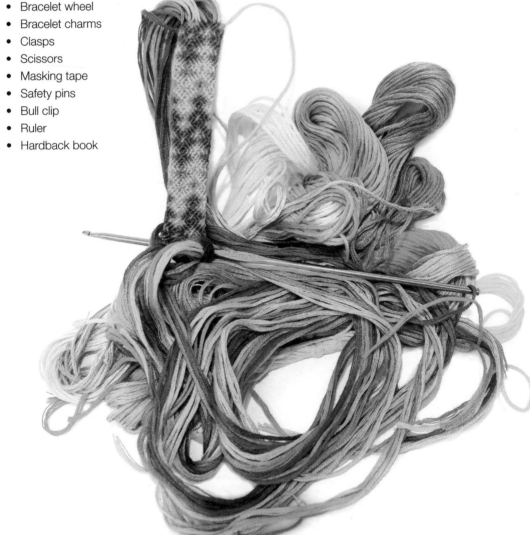

# Contents

# Beginnings

Knot-tying arts developed in different parts of the world. Some of the earliest decorative knots came from China. Over time, the Chinese developed many uses for knots, including clothing decoration, buttons and household objects.

Macrame, the craft of tying knots to create intricate patterns, is said to have developed in 13th-century Arabia. Arabian weavers are thought to have started creating knotted patterns with the fringe at the edges of items made on a loom. In later years, this practice travelled to Italy and France.

## What are friendship bracelets and where did they come from?

The art of making jewellery through weaving, braiding or knotting threads is a tradition that perhaps originated within the southern and central parts of America. This art has spread to many different cultures in many parts of the world.

Friendship bracelets are a symbol of friendship. The bands are made of thread, cotton and even beads in a variety of different colours and patterns and are a unique handmade gift. Friendship bracelets can be given to a special friend. You can add matching charms to your bracelets so you and your bestie bling in unison. Superstition says that this friendship will last as long as the bracelet stays on that special friend. If your friendship bracelet is somehow lost or ruined it's OK, so long as it hasn't been cut. Don't worry – you can always make another one.

## Uses

Friendship bracelets have a variety of different uses. They can be used for key rings, anklets, shoelaces, pet collars, zipper pulls, chokers and even hair ties. If you put your mind to it, we're sure you could come up with many other uses. Just let your imagination go!

# Patterns

This book contains patterns and instructions to create 11 different friendship bracelets. The last three designs require the use of a bracelet wheel. If you don't already have one you can follow the instructions on pages 47 and 48 to make your own.

## Stripy Stripy

## Beaded Knots

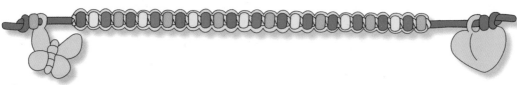

## Twister

## Beaded Plaits

## Surfin' Arrows

## Boardslide Arrows & Twists

## Beaded Arrows

## Gnarly Knots

## Four-thread Braid

## Round Braid

## Square Braid

# Getting Started

To get started you will need the following items:

- Coloured threads
- Scissors to cut threads
- Masking/sticky tape, a clipboard or a safety pin to hold your bracelet firmly in position
- Ruler
- Small packet of coloured beads
- Bracelet charms
- Clasps
- Bracelet wheel
- Bull clip
- Hardback book

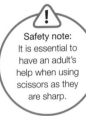

**Safety note:** It is essential to have an adult's help when using scissors as they are sharp.

There are three ways of keeping your bracelet firm whilst making it:

## Option 1

Stick tape over the ends of the thread. Then stick to a table or hardback book.

## Option 2

Clip the end of your bracelet to a clipboard or use a bull clip and attach it to a hardback book.

## Option 3

Push a safety pin through the knot at the beginning of your bracelet. Pin it to something sturdy, such as a chair or, if wearing jeans, your knee.

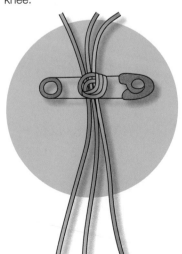

## Using Clasps

This book shows you how to make friendship bracelets with knotted ends. If you'd prefer a more polished finish you'll need to use clasps. Once your bracelet is finished, cut the loose the knotted threads at the start of the bracelet and the loose threads at the end. Place some glue at both ends of the bracelet to secure the threads. Once the glue has dried, press a clamp onto each end. The clamp will press into the threads and hold them. You can use pliers if you want to press the clamps more tightly. Slide a ring onto the end of each clamp, adding a clasp to one of them. You can now put your bracelet on your wrist!

## Adding Beads and Charms

The beauty of working with threads is that no matter the design, you can almost always add beads and charms to your bracelets whenever you like. The knots, plaits or braids will keep them in place as you continue making the bracelet. It's easiest to slide beads and charms onto single threads but they can be added to multiple threads (like in Beaded Arrows). Charms can also be easily added to the ring when attaching clasps.

## Friendship Bracelet Wheel

A friendship bracelet wheel can be used to make quick and simple bracelets for you and your friends. The wheel has 32 slots for your thread to be slid into. By placing the thread in the various slots you will be able to braid bracelets faster than ever before.

### BFF

Think about the friend you're making the bracelet for before you get started. What colours are their favourites? What pattern suits their personality? Which charm would they like best? After all, friendship bracelets are for your BFF.

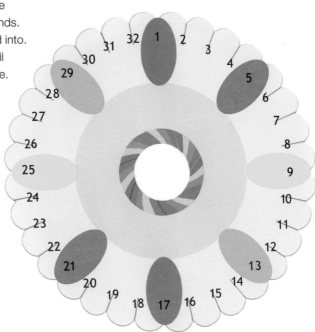

# Knotting Techniques

Before you start you must learn how to tie the basic knot that is used for all friendship bracelets. All you need to know is how to tie this knot in two different directions.

## Getting Started

First take two different coloured threads and tie them together. Stick, clip or pin your threads to keep them firm. The threads should be hanging side by side. Call the left-hand thread number 1 and the right-hand thread number 2. Follow these four easy steps and you're ready to begin.

## The basic left-hand knot

### Step 1

Hold thread 2 (right-hand thread) firmly and tie thread 1 (left-hand thread) around it.

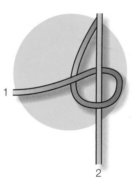

### Step 2

Pull thread 1 tight towards the left.

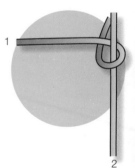

### Step 3

Repeat steps 1 and 2 to give you a double knot.

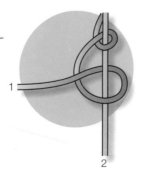

### Step 4

This is how your right to left knot should look. Always tie double knots!

# The basic right-hand knot

## Step 1

Hold thread 2 (right-hand thread) firmly and tie thread 1 (left-hand thread) around it.

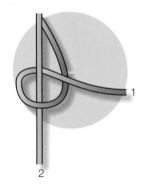

## Step 2

Pull thread 1 tight towards the right.

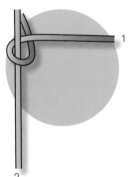

## Step 3

Repeat steps 1 and 2 to give you a double knot.

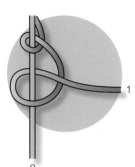

## Step 4

This is how your left to right knot should look. Always tie double knots!

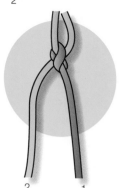

# Meaningful Colours

When choosing the threads and beads for each bracelet think about your friend and select colours that reflect their personality and character.

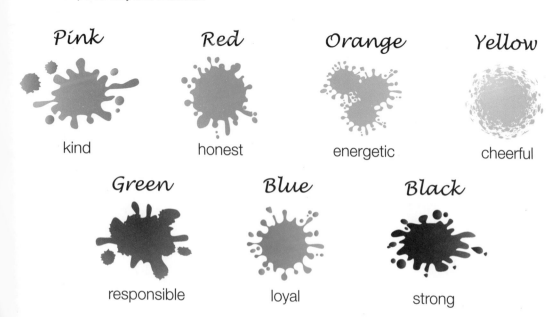

**Pink** — kind

**Red** — honest

**Orange** — energetic

**Yellow** — cheerful

**Green** — responsible

**Blue** — loyal

**Black** — strong

# Stripy Stripy

This whole bracelet is made with the basic left-hand knot. Once you have learnt this you can then move on to more complicated bracelets.

Select your choice of coloured threads. Stripy stripy is made with four coloured threads; however, to make your bracelet wider you can use as many threads as you like.

## Getting Started

Cut each thread about 60 cm (23.6 inches) long. Tie a knot about 5 cm (1.9 inches) from the top of your threads. Stick, clip or pin your threads to keep them firm. Separate your threads to make it easier for you to work with them.

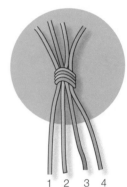

## Step 1

Starting with thread 1 (remember that's the left-hand thread), tie a left-hand knot over thread 2. Hold thread 2 firmly and pull thread 1 tight towards the left. Now repeat step 1 again to make a double knot.

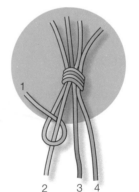
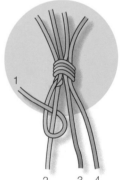

## Step 2

Take thread 1 and tie double knots around each of the remaining threads, moving from the left to the right.

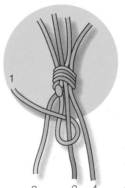
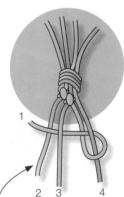

This is the thread you'll be working with next.

## Step 3

Repeat the same thing again. Start with the left-hand thread and tie double knots across all the different threads from left to right, until you have completed another row.

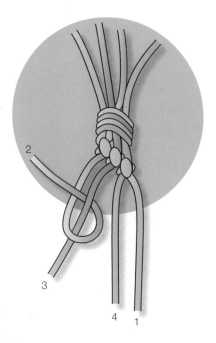

## Step 4

Continue tying knots until the bracelet is as long as you like, then tie a final knot. Leave about 10 cm (3.9 inches) of threads after the final knot and then cut the threads. The bracelet is now ready to give to a friend.

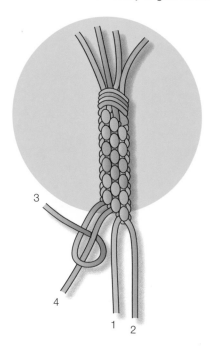

### Top Tip

If you want to get fancy with your bracelet, think about adding some beads. Just string them on between the knots. Or you can make the bracelet thicker by using more than four pieces of thread.

# Beaded Knots

This macrame style knotted bracelet is fun to make and incorporates beads and charms for a bold look.

## Getting Started

Choose two threads in two different colours. Cut 50 cm (20 inches) of one colour and 100 cm (40 inches) of the other. The longer colour will be the thread that is knotted and looped around the beads. Select approximately 30 beads and thread them onto the 50 cm thread, tying a knot at the top. You could also add a charm. Stick, clip or pin the 50 cm thread with the beads to keep it firm. Move the first bead to the knot at the top and leave 6 cm (2.4 inches) below it. Place the longer thread underneath the shorter thread at this point.

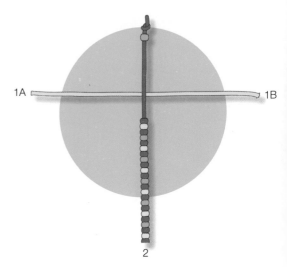

## Step 1

Bend thread 1A to the right so that it sits above thread 2 and goes under thread 1B.

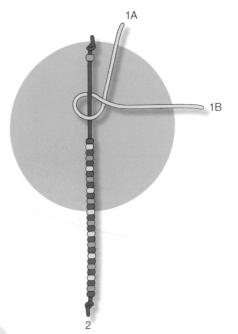

## Step 2

Bring thread 1B under thread 2 in the middle and through the loop. Tighten the knot.

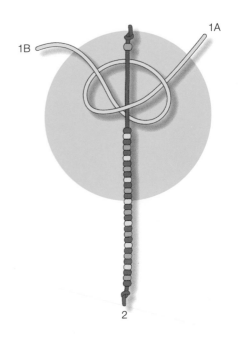

## Step 3

Bend thread 1B to the right so it goes under thread 2 and sits above thread 1A.

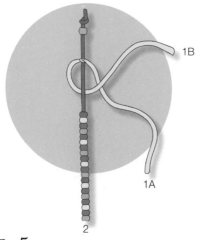

## Step 4

Bend thread 1A to the left across thread 2 and through the loop. Tighten the knot.

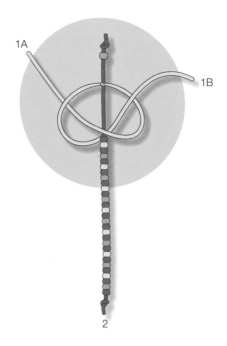

## Step 5

Move one bead up to this first knot. Repeat steps 1 to 4. Continue moving one bead at a time and repeating steps 1 to 4 until all the beads have been knotted.

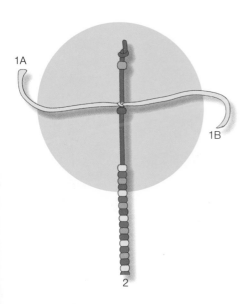

### Top Tip

If your bracelet starts to twist, you could tape the end of thread 2 down, keeping the bracelet nice and taut.

## Step 6

Cut any excess threads and tie a simple knot at the end of thread 2. Add a charm or two to either end of the bracelet. The bracelet is now ready to either tie to your wrist or finish with a clasp.

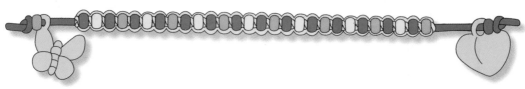

# Twister

This is another easy, quick and fun bracelet to make. Once you have mastered it, try using more threads to make an even thicker bracelet.

## Getting Started

Choose six threads in three colours (two threads in each colour). Cut each thread about 60 cm (23.6 inches) long. Tie a knot about 5 cm (1.9 inches) from the top of your threads. Stick, clip or pin your threads to keep them firm.

## Step 1

Collect all threads together in a bunch, leaving one thread out (thread 1).

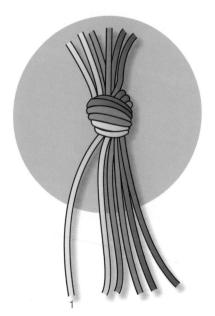

## Step 2

Tie a basic left-hand knot with thread 1 around the bunch. Repeat this 10 times, making sure the knots are pulled tight towards the left each time.

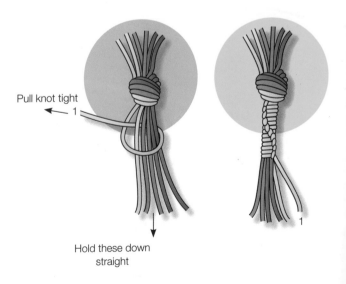

Pull knot tight

Hold these down straight

## Step 3

Separate the threads into three different bunches,
one bunch of each colour, so you now have
two threads of the same colour in each bunch.

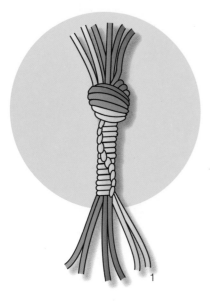

## Step 4

Plait the three bunches until the plaited part
of the bracelet is as long as the knotted part.

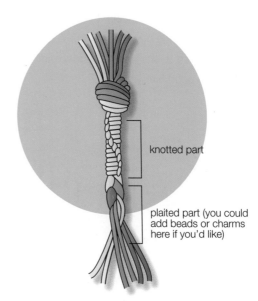

knotted part

plaited part (you could
add beads or charms
here if you'd like)

## Step 5

Collect all the threads together again, this time
leaving one thread out and making sure it is a
different colour to the thread used in step 1.
This thread will now be called thread 1.

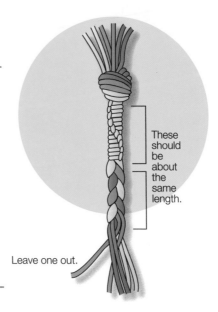

These
should
be
about
the
same
length.

Leave one out.

## Step 6

Repeat steps 2–5 until the bracelet is as long as you
like, then tie a final knot. Leave about 10 cm (3.9
inches) of threads after the final knot and then cut the
threads. The bracelet is now ready to give to a friend.

# Beaded Plaits

This is another very easy bracelet to make.
All you need to know is how to plait, then just
add some coloured beads or fun charms, and
your bracelet is complete!

Plaiting a friendship bracelet uses the
same technique as plaiting your hair.

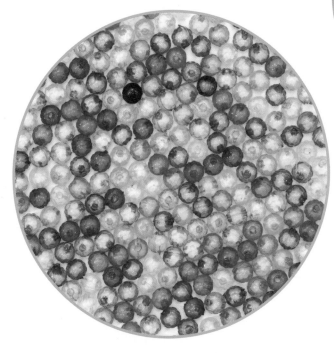

## Beads and threads

Beads come in all shapes and sizes!
If the hole in your bead is too small for
the string you are using, try splitting off
a couple of threads to make it thinner.
You can also wet and twist the
thread end to make it easier
to thread beads.

## Getting Started

Choose three different colours, four threads of
each colour. Cut each thread about 60 cm (23.6
inches) long. Tie a knot about 5 cm (1.9 inches)
from the top of your threads. Stick, clip or pin your
threads to keep them firm.

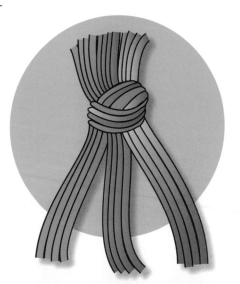

## Step 1

Separate the threads into three different bunches, one for each of the three colours, so you have four threads of the same colour in each bunch.

Now start plaiting: you just have to cross the right-hand bunch over the middle bunch and then the left-hand bunch over the middle bunch. Remember, the middle bunch will always change.

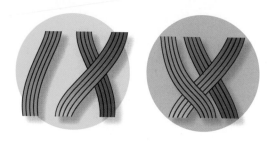

## Step 2

Now it's time to add your beads. One at a time, thread a single bead onto one of your threads every second time it becomes your left-side bunch. Make sure you always put the bead on the same coloured thread each time.

## Step 3

Continue plaiting until the bracelet is as long as you like, then tie a final knot. Leave about 10 cm (3.9 inches) of threads after the final knot and then cut the threads. The bracelet is now ready to give to a friend.

### Top Tip

Storing your beads is important because it's so easy to drop and lose them. You can buy small storage containers for beads at most craft stores. You can also store them in old clean jars or shampoo bottles. Old clean spice jars are particularly good for bead storage.

# Surfin' Arrows

Friendship bracelets are big in today's surf scene with both guys and girls. Surfing buddies wear bracelets of all colours and styles and they look really cool when done in the same colours as your friend's surf gear!

This bracelet is made using both the basic left-hand and basic right-hand knots shown on pages 10 and 11. This pattern is used in many of the other bracelets so make sure you feel comfortable with it before you try the more difficult ones. For the surf scene, blue, red, yellow and green look good.

## Getting Started

Choose four different-coloured threads. Cut each thread about 130 cm (51.1 inches) long. Fold the threads in half and tie a knot about 5 cm (1.9 inches) from the top of your threads, making a loop. Now you will have eight threads, two of each colour. Stick, clip or pin your threads to keep them firm. Separate your threads and arrange them in the order shown.

1 2 3 4    4 3 2 1

## Step 1

Tie a basic left-hand knot using the first thread (number 1) around each of threads 2, 3 and 4, moving from left to right and stopping in the middle. Remember to always tie double knots.

1

2 3 4    4 3 2 1

# Step 2

Take the first thread (number 1) on the right side and again move towards the middle, tying basic right-hand double knots around each of threads 2, 3 and 4.

2 3  4 1  4  3

# Step 3

Your bracelet should now look like the picture, with the two thread 1s in the middle. Using a basic right-hand knot, tie these two middle thread 1s together, making sure that you pull the knot tight towards the right.

2 3  4 1 1 4  3 2         2 3  4 1 1 4  3 2

# Step 4

Repeat steps 1–3, always beginning with the outside threads left and right and working towards the middle. When your bracelet is at the desired length, tie a final knot. Leave about 10 cm (3.9 inches) of threads after the final knot and then cut the threads. The bracelet is now ready to give to a friend.

## Top Tip

Make sure all of your knots are tight so that the design is clear. Always double knot your thread. Your bracelet will look a little odd in any spots where you miss the double knot.

# Boardslide Arrows & Twists

A boardslide is a medium-difficulty skateboard move and this bracelet is medium difficulty to make! Try making one for a friend in the same colours as their skateboard.

## Getting Started

Make sure you have practised the Surfin' Arrows bracelet on pages 20 and 21 before you attempt this one. Again choose four different colours. Cut each thread about 150 cm (59.1 inches) long. Fold the threads in half and tie a knot about 5 cm (1.9 inches) from the top of your threads, making a loop. Now you will have eight threads, two of each colour. Stick, clip or pin your threads to keep them firm. Separate your threads and arrange them in the order shown here.

## Step 1

Make a Surfin' Arrow just like you did on pages 20 and 21. Using thread 1, tie a basic left-hand double knot around threads 2, 3 and 4, moving into the middle from left to right.

## Step 2

Take the first thread on the right side (thread 1) and again move towards the middle, tying basic right-hand double knots around threads 2, 3 and 4.

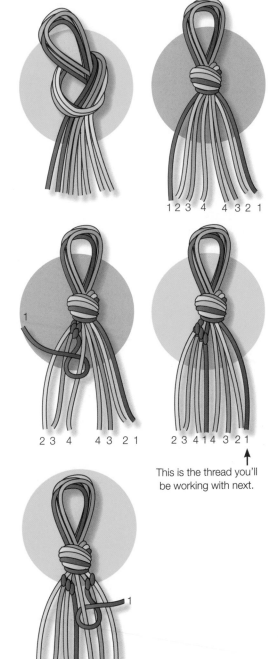

1 2 3  4    4 3 2 1

2 3  4    4 3 2 1

2 3 4 1 4 3 2 1

↑
This is the thread you'll be working with next.

2 3  4 1 4 3 2

## Step 3

Your bracelet should now look like this with
the two thread 1s in the middle.

Again using a basic right-hand knot tie these
two middle thread 1s together, making sure that
you pull the knot tight towards the right.

2 3  4 11 4  3 2          2 3  4 11 4  3 2

## Step 4

Repeat steps 1–3 another three times so you
have one Surfin' Arrow in all four colours.
Make sure you always begin with the outside
threads left and right and work towards the middle.
Your threads will now be in the same order as
when you started.

1 2  3 4 4 3 2 1

## Step 5

Collect threads 2, 3 and 4 on the left side, leaving
thread 1 out. Next tie a single basic left-hand
knot with thread 1 around threads 2, 3 and 4.
Repeat this 10 times, making sure the knots
are pulled tight towards the left each time.

2 3 4   4 3 2 1          2 3 4 1   4 3 2 1

## Step 6

Now do the same thing with the right-hand side. Collect threads 2, 3 and 4 on the right side, again leaving thread 1 out, then tie a basic right-hand single knot with thread 1 around threads 2, 3 and 4. Repeat this 10 times as in step 5.

2 3 4 1     4 3 2          2 3 4 1     1 4 3 2

## Step 7

More Surfin' Arrows! Repeat steps 1–5, this time starting with your new number 1 threads, which will now be a different colour. (These thread number 1s will be the same colour as the second Surfin' Arrow that you have just done.)

1 2 3 4     4 3 2 1

## Step 8

Continue this pattern until the bracelet is as long as you like, then tie a final knot. Leave about 10 cm (3.9 inches) of threads after the final knot and then cut the threads. The bracelet is now ready to give to a friend.

### Top Tip

Experiment with different jewellery clips and clasps to finish your friendship bracelets. They are available from most craft stores and will give your bracelets a fancy finish.

# Beaded Arrows

This is probably one of the most difficult patterns in this book so make sure you're prepared. Once again, it mostly uses the Surfin' Arrows, but also adds beads and a border around your bracelet.

## Getting Started

Choose four different colours. Cut each thread about 150 cm (59.1 inches) long. Fold the threads in half and tie a knot about 5 cm (1.9 inches) from the top of your threads, making a loop. Now you will have eight threads, two of each colour. Stick, clip or pin your threads to keep them firm. Separate your threads and arrange them in the order shown here.

1 2 3 4    4 3 2 1

## Step 1

Start with the first thread 1, on the left side. Tie a single basic left-hand knot around thread 2. Now tie another single knot with the same thread 1. This time tie a single basic right-hand knot around thread 2. This completes the first knots in the left side of your border.

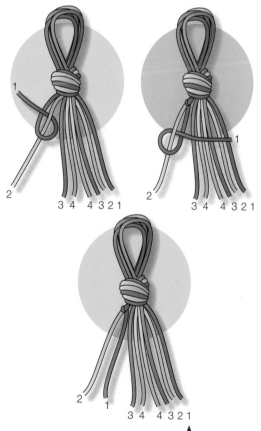

This is the thread you'll be using for the next two steps.

## Step 2

With the first thread 1 on the right side, tie a single basic right-hand knot around thread 2. Then tie a single basic left-hand knot with the same thread around thread 2, making sure you pull the threads tight each time. The threads again will be in their original order. Put both left and right thread 1s out of the way as you will not need them again for a few steps.

## Step 3

Now you will be using only threads 2, 3 and 4 on both sides. First tie a double basic left-hand knot with the left thread 2 around thread 3 and then around thread 4, moving towards the middle. Then tie a double basic right-hand knot with the right side thread 2 around threads 3 and 4.

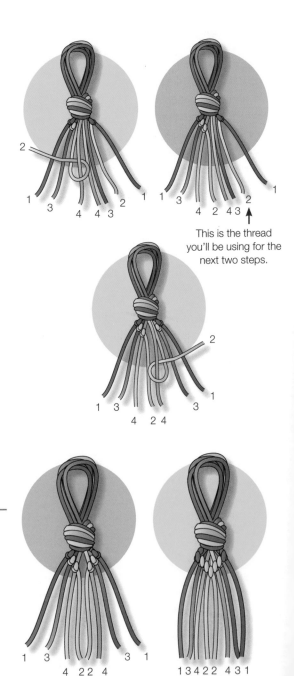

This is the thread you'll be using for the next two steps.

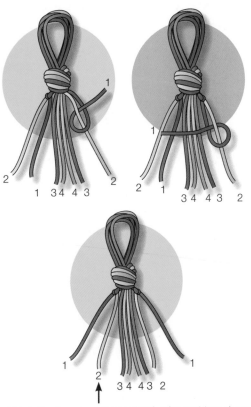

This is the thread you'll be using for the next two steps.

## Step 4

Tie both thread 2s together using a double basic right-hand knot.

## Step 5

Repeat steps 1–4 until you have made six bordered Surfin' Arrows. Choose 2–3 beads and thread them onto the two middle thread 4s.

1 2 3 4 4   3 2 1

## Step 6

You will now be working with one side of the bracelet at a time (left side first). Again using thread 1 (the thread which you put to the side), tie a single basic left-hand knot around thread 2 and then tie a basic right-hand knot using the same threads to make another border.

1 2  3 4 4  3 2 1

## Step 7

Using thread 2, tie a basic left-hand double knot around thread 3, pulling thread 2 towards the left. Make sure you keep thread 3 nice and tight. Repeat steps 6 and 7 until your borders are as long as your beads.

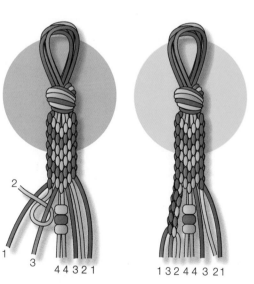

## Step 8

Now do the same thing to the right side of the
bracelet. Using thread 1 on the right side, tie a
single basic right-hand knot around thread 2 and
then tie a basic left-hand knot using the same
threads to make another border. Using thread 2,
tie a basic right-hand double knot around thread 3,
pulling thread 2 towards the right. Make sure you
keep thread 3 nice and tight. Repeat step 8 until
your borders are as long as your beads.

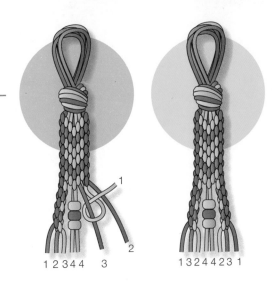

## Step 9

Repeat steps 1–8. Remember to always work
with the left side of your bracelet first. Continue this
pattern until the bracelet is as long as you like, then
tie a final knot. Leave about 10 cm (3.9 inches) of
threads after the final knot and then cut the threads.
The bracelet is now ready to give to a friend.

## Top Tip

It looks great when you use beads
that are the same colour as your
thread colours. Alternatively, you can
choose beads that are much brighter
than your thread colours if you want
them to stand out.

# Gnarly Knots

Surfers describe difficult or dangerous waves as 'gnarly'. You won't be in any danger trying out this cool design, but it is a little bit challenging, so make sure you're comfortable with the Beaded Knots bracelet before you start this one.

## Getting Started

Choose three threads in three different colours, and cut 200 cm (80 inches) of two of them and 50 cm (20 inches) of the third. Fold the two longer threads (1 and 2) in half. Align one end of the shorter thread (3) with the folded ends of the longer threads and tie a knot, making a loop. Now you will have five threads. Stick, clip or pin your threads to keep them firm. Separate your threads and arrange them in the order shown here.

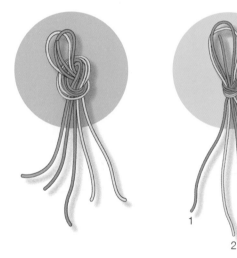

## Step 1

Select approximately 20 beads and thread them onto thread 3. Then choose one end of both longer threads, line them up with thread 3, and use tape to stick down the ends of these three threads to keep them firm.

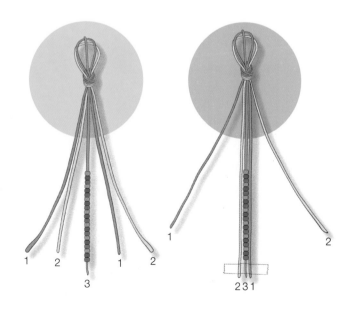

29

# Step 2

Bend thread 1 to the right, under the three middle threads, and lay it over thread 2. Then bring thread 2 to the left, over the three middle threads and under the loop of thread 1. Tighten the knot.

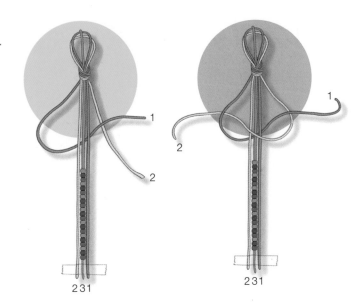

# Step 3

Bring thread 1 back to the left, under the three middle threads, and lay it over thread 2. Then bring thread 2 back to the right, over the three middle threads and under the loop of thread 1. Tighten the knot.

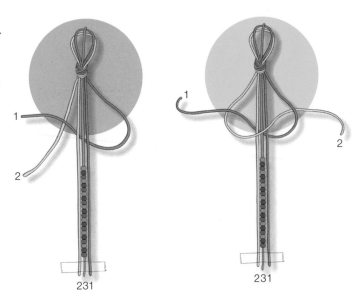

## Top Tip

This is one of the hardest friendship bracelet designs in this book, so don't be discouraged if things go wrong. Take your time and keep trying. Your friend is worth the effort.

Masking tape helps to hold the beaded section of the design in place while you create the rest of the bracelet.

## Step 4

Repeat steps 2-3 until you have about 3 cm (1.2 in)
of knots (around 10 knots). Make sure you pass the
same thread under the three middle threads every
time, and the other thread over the three middle
threads every time, otherwise your pattern won't
be consistent. After about 10 knots, repeat step 2,
but not step 3. This means that you'll only be tying
half of one knot, so that thread 1 ends up on the
right and thread 2 ends up on the left. Then release
the other ends of threads 1 and 2 from the middle
section. Make sure thread 3 stays taped down, and
be careful not to lose any beads! Then align both of
your thread 1s side by side and both of your thread
2s side by side.

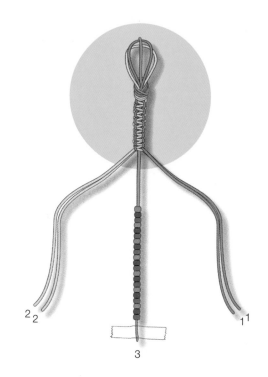

## Step 5

Bend both thread 1s to the left, under thread 3 in
the middle, and lay them over your thread 2s. Then
bring your thread 2s to the right, over the middle
thread and under the loop of your thread 1s.
Tighten the knot.

## Step 6

Move one bead up to this knot, then repeat steps
2-3 with both of your thread 1s and both of your
thread 2s.

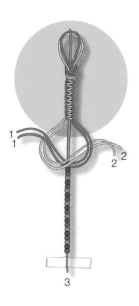

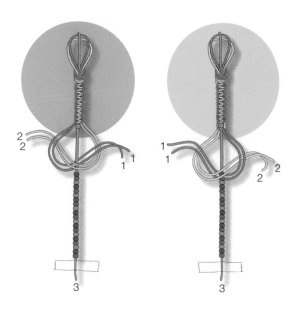

## Step 7

If you want to add charms to your bracelet, thread them onto both of your thread 1s or both of your thread 2s when you move a new bead up towards the knot, then continue with the knot and tighten to secure the charm in place.

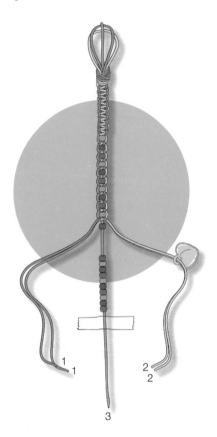

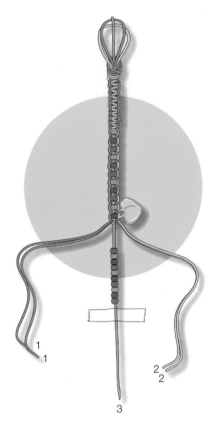

## Step 8

Repeat step 6 until all beads except one have been knotted. When you move your last bead up to the knot, repeat step 2 (but not step 3) with both of your thread 1s and both of your thread 2s. Then choose one of your thread 1s and one of your thread 2s, move them into the middle section alongside thread 3, and tape down these three threads firmly. One of your thread 1s will be slightly shorter than the other, because you've already worked with this one. It's best to stick the shorter thread 1 down with thread 3. The same applies to your thread 2s.

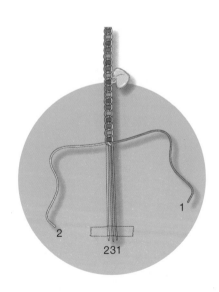

## Step 9

Bring the other thread 1 under the three
middle threads and lay it over thread 2.
Then bring thread 2 over the three middle
threads and under the loop of thread 1.
Tighten the knot.

1

2

2 3 1

## Step 10

Repeat steps 2-3 until you have about 3 cm (1.2 in) of knots (probably about 10 knots).
Then tie a simple knot and tighten it so that it sits a close as possible to your last knot.
Leave about 10 cm (3.9 inches) of thread after the final knot and then cut the thread. The
bracelet is now ready to tie to your wrist (or your BFF's), or finish with a clasp!

# Friendship Bracelet Wheel

A friendship bracelet wheel is a useful tool to help you make braided friendship bracelets. Friendship bracelet wheels are also called kumihimo wheels. Kumihimo is a Japanese method of braiding. *Kumi himo* is Japanese for 'gathered threads'.

## History

Braiding silk and thread has been part of many cultures throughout history. The Japanese began braiding cord and silk for Samurai warriors to lace and decorate their armour.

Braiding later developed into a decorative way of fastening kimonos. The Japanese developed methods that allowed for braids to become very complex and intricate. With more advanced methods came more decorative braids, until each braid was so unique that it became a symbol of a Japanese warrior's status.

Braiding can be used as a decorative way to fasten a kimono.

Friendship wheels allow us to braid bracelets giving similar results to hair braids.

## Top Tip

Numbering the slots on the friendship bracelet wheel from 1 to 32 makes it easier to follow the patterns. You can also use a pencil to write which colour goes into which slot for a specific design. You could then erase these colour notations once you're finished with that design.

# Bracelet Wheel

The friendship bracelet wheel acts as a loom and braiding guide. In no time at all you will begin to see your braided bracelet taking shape. Make sure you hold the knotted thread ends tight through the wheel. It might take a little bit of practice but soon you will develop a rhythm and your bracelet will be ready in no time.

# Slotting and Twisting

Most designs for the bracelet wheel involve threading the colours through the different slots. You then twist the wheel around and move each colour to a different slot. It's really easy and so quick!

# Clasp Finish

You can use clasps to finish bracelets made on the friendship wheel. Simply cut the knotted end off and apply some glue to both ends. Press a clamp onto each end of the bracelet once the glue has dried. Add a ring to the end of each clamp and a clasp to one of the rings. A charm can be added to either ring.

## Top Tip

The way the colours are strung on the bracelet wheel determines where the colours will show up in the braid.

# Adding Beads

Beads can be added to your bracelets by simply sliding them onto the thread when you are moving it. Try to add beads in even spacings.

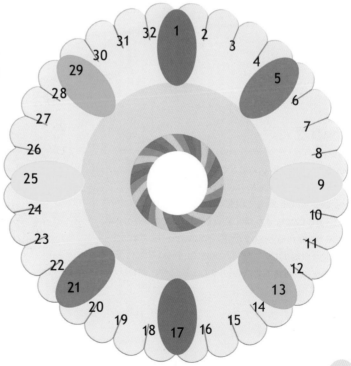

# Four-thread Braid

A four-thread braid is the simplest braid you can create on the bracelet wheel. It makes a thin twisted braid. You can double the length of the threads you use and wrap the finished bracelet around your wrist twice.

## Getting Started

You need four coloured threads of about 30 cm (11.8 inches) each. Gather all the threads together and tie a knot about 5 cm (1.9 inches) from the top.

It can be helpful to think of your friendship wheel like the face of a clock.

## Step 1

Feed the knotted threads through the hole in the centre of the bracelet wheel and hold them firmly at the back of the wheel.

## Step 2

Set your threads up so that they are evenly spaced and opposite each other. Imagine the bracelet wheel as a clock. You want thread slotting into 12 o'clock, 3 o'clock, 6 o'clock and 9 o'clock. If you have numbered slots, you want the thread through positions 1, 9, 17 and 25. Hold the knotted threads tightly at the back of the wheel.

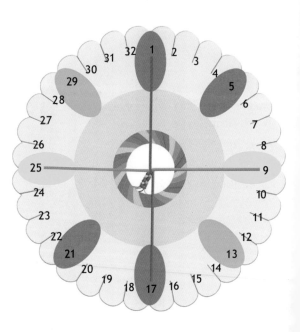

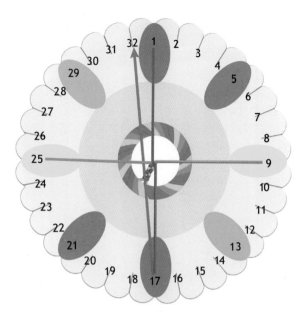

## Step 3

Move the bottom thread up to the slot to the left of the top thread (position number 32).

## Step 4

Move the top thread down to the 6 o'clock position (position number 17). Move what is now the top thread to position 1.

### Top Tip

Run your fingers through the hanging threads if they get tangled.

## Step 5

Move the left thread to the right and slot into the groove above the 3 o'clock position (position number 8).

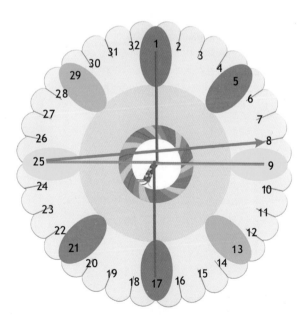

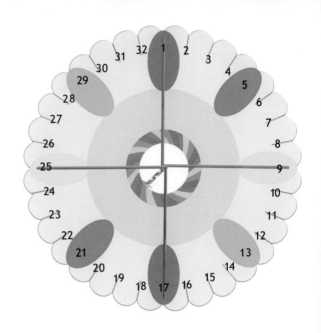

## Step 6

Move the right thread to the left so it's at the 9 o'clock position (position number 25). Move what is now the right thread to position 9.

## Step 7

Repeat steps 3–6 until your bracelet has reached your desired length. There is no need to turn the wheel in this simple braided bracelet. You simply repeat the steps over and over. It might be necessary to twist the braided bracelet together as you repeat the steps. This also helps to keep the threads nice and tight.

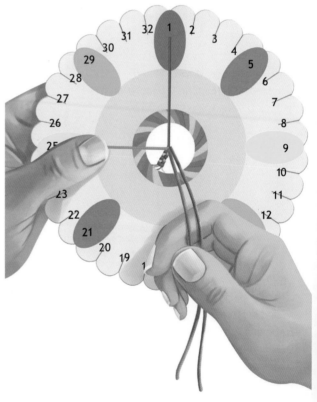

## Step 8

Remove the threads from the wheel and tie a final knot. Leave about 5 cm (1.9 inches) of threads after the final knot and then cut the threads. The bracelet is now ready to give to a friend.

# Round Braid

A round braid is made with four coloured threads. It is a very pretty bracelet design and is quick and easy to make.

## Getting Started

You need two lengths of each colour. Divide each colour into equal lengths of about 40 cm (15.8 inches) long. Gather all the threads together and tie a knot about 5 cm (1.9 inches) from the top.

This pattern involves turning the wheel as you follow it so that you are always working from top to bottom. This makes it easier to keep track of which thread is next.

### Top Tip

Make sure you don't cross the warps (for example taking a left strand from the bottom and placing it on the upper right).

## Step 1

Feed the threads through the hole in the centre of the bracelet wheel and hold them firmly at the back of the wheel.

## Step 2

The aim when setting your threads up on the wheel is to have pairs of the same coloured threads at the top, bottom, left and right sides of the wheel. If you have a numbered wheel then threads of the same colour should be slotted through positions 1 and 32, 8 and 9, 16 and 17 and 24 and 25.

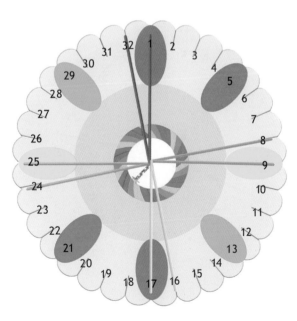

## Step 3

Starting with the number 1 slot at the top, bring the top right thread (the one in position 1) to the bottom right (position 15).

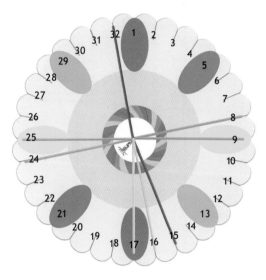

## Step 4

Bring the bottom left thread (position 17) up to the top left (position 31).

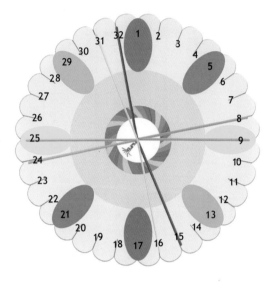

## Step 5

Rotate the board 90 degrees clockwise so the threads at positions 24 and 25 are at the top. Bring the top right thread (the one in position 25) down to the bottom right (position 7).

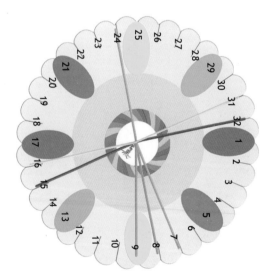

## Step 6

Bring the bottom left thread (the one in position 9) up to the top left (position 23).

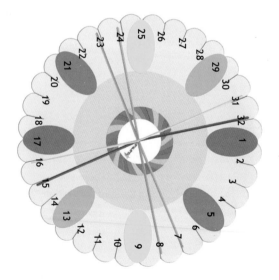

## Step 7

Rotate the board 90 degrees clockwise.
Bring the top right thread (the one in position 16)
to the bottom right (position 30).

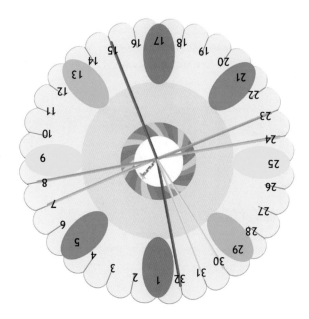

## Step 8

Bring the bottom left thread (position 32)
up to the top left (position 14).

## Step 9

Rotate the board 90 degrees clockwise and
continue the pattern. The number positions will
change as you continue around the wheel but just
keep the pattern in mind. An easy way to remember
it is to say to yourself, 'Right down, left up. Turn.'

## Step 10

Continue the pattern until the bracelet has
reached your desired length.

# Step 11

Remove the threads from the wheel and tie a final knot. Leave about 5 cm (1.9 inches) of threads after the final knot and then cut the threads. The bracelet is now ready to give to a friend.

# Variation

You can use this pattern with more threads if you like. The more threads you use, the thicker the bracelet will be. Just make sure the pairs of threads are spread evenly around the wheel.

## Top Tip

If your long loose threads hanging from the wheel keep getting tangled, gather each of them and tie them into a loose knot. This way they will be shorter and more manageable. Release more thread as you need it.

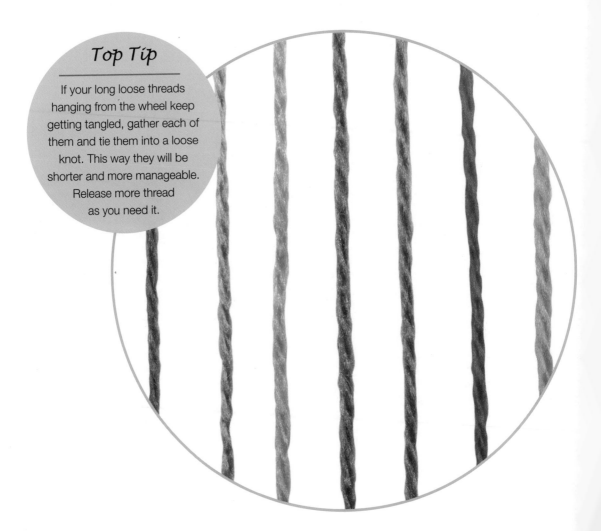

# Square Braid

Creating a square braided bracelet using a bracelet wheel is a little tricky. It will become easier once you get the hang of it though, so don't give up.

## Getting Started

A square braid is made with threads of four different colours. You need four lengths of each colour. Divide each colour into equal lengths of about 45 cm (17.7 inches) long. Gather all 16 threads together and tie a knot about 5 cm (1.9 inches) from the top.

### Top Tip

For an interesting effect, arrange two colours in each group with the darker colour on the inside. When your braid is complete the darker colours will appear on one side and the lighter colours on the other.

## Step 1

Feed the knotted thread through the hole in the centre of the bracelet wheel and hold it firmly at the back of the wheel.

## Step 2

The aim when setting your threads up on the wheel is to have pairs of the same coloured threads at the top, bottom, left and right sides of the wheel. If you have a numbered wheel that means threads of the same colour slotted through positions 32, 1, 2, 3 and 8, 9, 10, 11 and 16, 17, 18, 19 and 24, 25, 26 and 27.

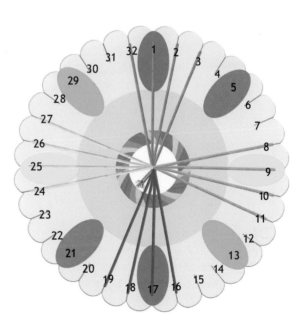

## Step 3

Take the two inner threads from the top (positions 1 and 2) and move them to the outer bottom slots (positions 15 and 20).

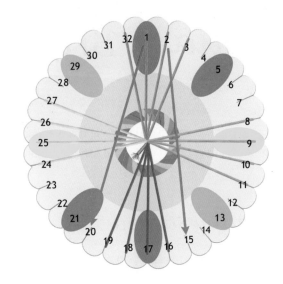

## Step 4

Take the two inner threads from the bottom (positions 17 and 18) and move them to the outer slots at the top (positions 4 and 31).

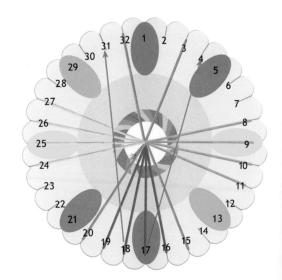

## Step 5

Move all four threads at the top inwards one slot (so they are now at positions 32, 1, 2 and 3).

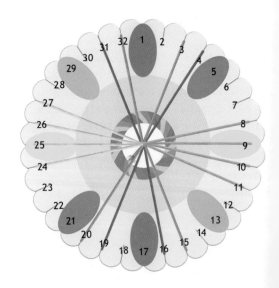

## Step 6

Move all four threads at the bottom inwards one slot (so they are now at positions 16, 17, 18 and 19).

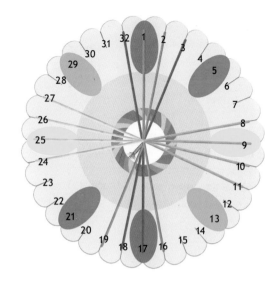

## Step 7

Rotate the board anti-clockwise so the threads at positions 8, 9, 10 and 11 are now at the top.

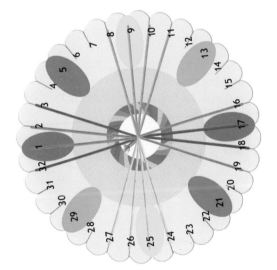

## Step 8

Repeat steps 3–6 and continue to follow the pattern. An easy way to remember it is to say to yourself, 'Inner to outer, inner to outer. In, in. In, in. Turn.'

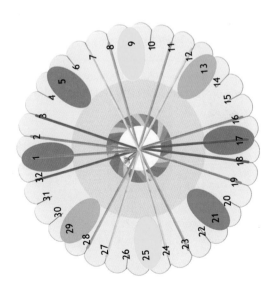

## Step 9

Continue the pattern until the bracelet has reached your desired length.

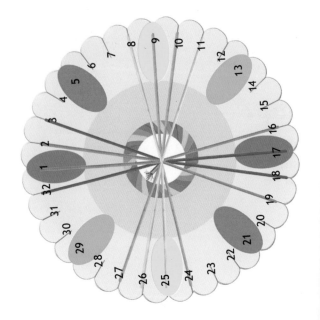

## Step 10

Remove the threads from the wheel and tie a final knot. Leave about 5 cm (1.9 inches) of threads after the final knot and then cut the threads. The bracelet is now ready to give to a friend.

## Rainbow-coloured Square Braid

To make a rainbow-coloured square braid follow the colours and positions shown to the right.

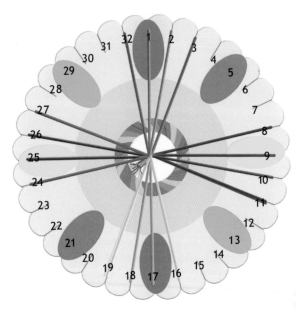

### Top Tip

Try to ensure that you pull the threads tight in a consistent way. Any looser threads will create bumps in your bracelet.

# Make Your Own Wheel

You can never have too many friendship bracelet wheels. It's good to work on lots of different patterns at the same time so when you get tired of one you can move on to another. Or you and your friends can use them at the same time to make each other bracelets.

## You Will Need :

- The template on page 48
- Cardboard
- Scissors
- Glue

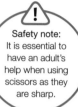

Safety note:
It is essential to have an adult's help when using scissors as they are sharp.

### Top Tip

If you want to make a stronger bracelet wheel, glue the template onto thick foam instead of cardboard.

## How to Make Your Own Wheel

1. Photocopy the bracelet wheel template on page 48.

2. Cut out the template and glue it onto the cardboard.

3. Wait for the glue to dry and then cut the template out of the cardboard.

4. Cutting out the inner circle is a little difficult so ask an adult for help with this.

5. Your new bracelet wheel is ready for use.

### Top Tip

Using different colours or even just setting up the threads in a different order can give a very different look to your braided friendship bracelets.

## Square Plate

You can also use kumihimo square plates to create braided friendship bracelets. Look online or in craft stores to find them. The square plate means the finished bracelet is quite flat.

# Make Your Own Wheel

Photocopy this wheel and follow the instructions on page 47 to make your own bracelet wheel.

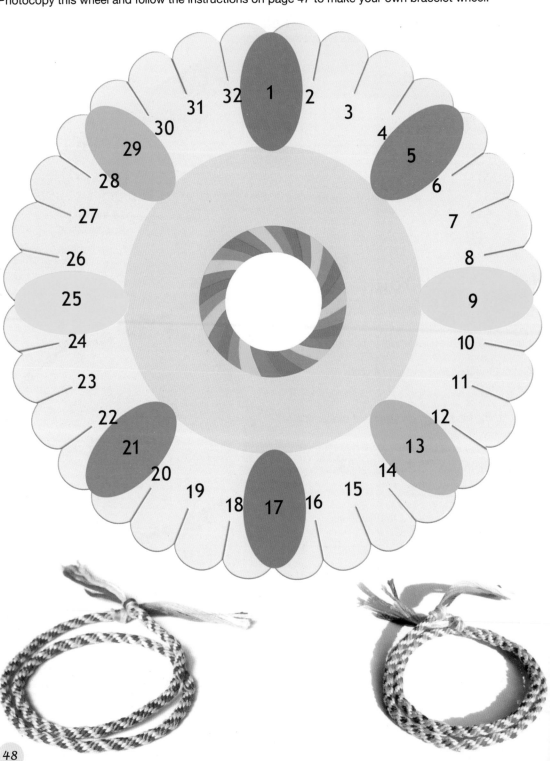